THE PALACE OF TH...
LOST CIT...

AT SUN CITY

Republic of Bophuthatswana, Southern Africa

SOUVENIR BROCHURE

CONTENTS

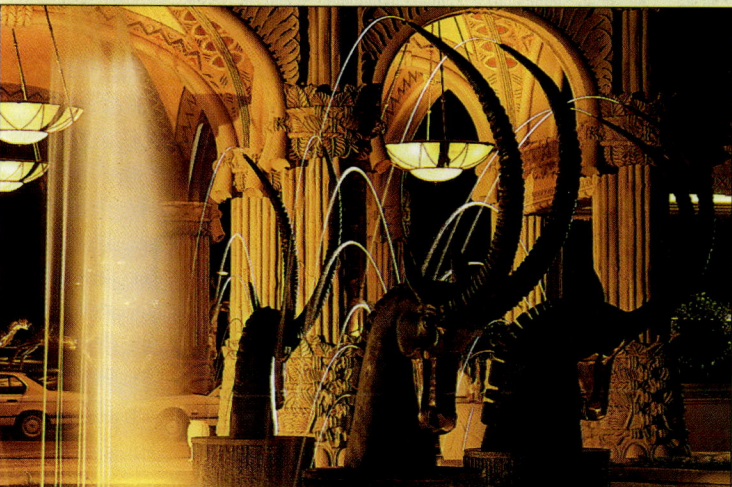

The Lost City at Sun City pays homage to art, architecture and nature. From the beach of the Valley of Waves to the soaring towers of The Palace, it lies at peace under a blue sky (above).

Welcome to The Palace (left). Step into a world of legendary hospitality, where age-old craftsmanship has sculpted a tribute to the creatures of the wild, cooled by the spray of fountains and lulled by the whisper of breezes through palm fronds.

A sweep of sable horns frames the gathering dusk over the porte-cochère, while leopards stand sentinel on the rooftop (above). Frightened buck, captured in bronze, leap to escape the outstretched claws of that swiftest of night-time hunters, the cheetah (right).

THE LEGEND
OF THE LOST CITY

Centuries before tall ships were ever dreamed about and long before the dawn of a western civilisation, nomadic people from northern Africa set out to seek a new world. Eventually they found a land of peace and plenty in a secluded valley, shaped by an ancient volcanic crater. The gold these people mined brought them great riches, and they built a mighty Palace for their benevolent king, whose hospitality became renowned throughout Africa. But one terrible day an earthquake destroyed their homes, aquaducts, fields and mine shafts, sparing only the Palace on its foundations of rock, and the people fled. Vegetation slowly concealed the ruins until all that remained was a memory, the legend of a Lost City. . .until in 1991 it was 'rediscovered' at Sun City and restored to its former splendour by the following year. A new era of hospitality had begun in an exciting and amazing leisure resort.

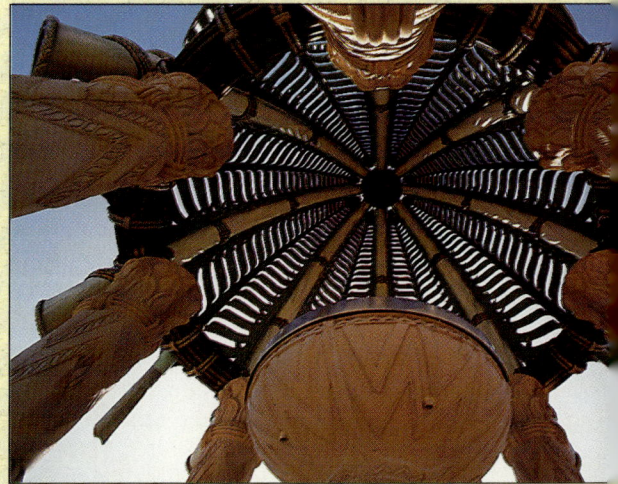

THE PALACE OF THE LOST CITY

Today The Palace *(below, and opposite page)* offers royal hospitality to guests from all over the world. It is the jewel in the crown of The Lost City, with each of the 338 magnificent en-suite rooms decorated with unique individuality and luxury. The Royal Entrance Chamber beyond the porte-cochère is breathtaking. Colonnades of bamboo and palm fronds, resting on elephant feet, appear to be carved from stone. They soar 25 metres from the intricate mosaic floor to a frescoed rotunda, where animals stalk the plains of Africa, bathed in the golden light of the midday sun. Beyond, a graceful staircase of rock crystal, bronze and marble flows down into the Crystal Court, a restaurant of lofty arches and jewelled mosaics, overlooking the Valley of Waves. In the Villa del Palazzo, where the art of fine dining has been perfected, elegant frescos curve across cupola ceilings in five separate pavilions. Deep glass windows fold back to give views across the Grand Pool.

Faux elephant tusks and graceful ferns weave together to create the impressive domes of The Palace (left, top and bottom). On one of them, a sacred flame still burns to proclaim peace in the Valley. It was from these vantage points that the king's lookouts heralded the arrival of important visitors, and watched the movement of game.

![elephant icon]

THE PALACE INTERIOR

The ancient people who built this Palace for their ruler, drew for its design on memories of their northern African heritage, and the animals and plants they found in their tranquil valley. Mightiest of them all was the elephant. So, the elephant is king—from the Crystal Court's imposing fountain, held aloft by four elephants whose trunks curl over their backs to spray water into the bronze bowl *(far right, top and centre)*, to the supremely comfortable Tusk Bar and Lounge and imposing Elephant Walk *(above)*, protected from the elements by a glass roof.

One of the most unforgettable
works of art in The Palace is the
Leonardo da Vinci-style frescoed dome of the 25-metre-high
entrance rotunda (centre). It is
16 metres in diameter, with an
oculus at the centre, encircled
by a painting in six sections
which took nearly 5 000 hours
to complete. Painstaking brush-
work has created a fantasy
jungle of animals whose story-
book ancestry includes cheetah,
zebra, waterbuck, nyala and
monkey.

Architraves, cornices and skirtings are made from 'cast'
stone to appear as if weathered by centuries of wind and
water, but the mosaic floor (centre) has been 'restored'
to perfection. It contains 300 000 pieces of marble and
granite in 38 shades, hand-laid and hand-polished in
a grand design.

Serving regional Italian cuisine, the dramatic Villa del Palazzo restaurant has been designed in the form of five domed pavilions. Clerestory windows overlook the Grand Pool, and the chairs are hand-carved with representations of various wild animals (left, top).

Stand in the Crystal Court (right), with its impressive colonnades and seven-metre-high doors opening onto rolling views over the Valley of Waves, and each fresh angle highlights some new and exciting accent of its golden interior.

DINING IN STYLE

Fine cuisine, perfect settings and excellent service make dining at The Palace a special occasion.

Art mirrors nature in a myriad of design accents throughout The Palace, and everywhere guests can relax and refresh themselves in sumptuous surroundings. Graceful palm fronds carved by artists and rustling, green fronds fashioned by Nature herself decorate the Palm Court Lounge (above), perfect for pre-lunch cocktails and after-dinner reminiscing. Cool and beautiful, the lounge has river-polished pebble walls, a unique hand-poured mosaic floor, and cast-stone, fluted columns whose creamy palm fronds form architraves against a delicately frescoed ceiling.

THE KING'S SUITE

The Palace offers accommodation to suit all tastes, but the most opulent is the King's Suite *(below)*, which has maple panelling, a delicate fresco on the drawing room ceiling, objets d'art scattered among the leather-bound volumes in the private library—and glass walls to one of the large bathrooms, providing a starscape by night and a stunning panorama over The Lost City by day.

The ancient ruins of an amphitheatre are reflected in the ripples of the Royal Baths (right), connected to The Palace by the king's Royal Staircase, which can be seen rising in the distance.

SPECTACULAR POOLS

The Grand Pool at The Palace is another expression of the legends of The Lost City, for the mosaics beneath the water tell an age-old story about two warring suns, Los and Nus. It is flanked on one side by a hill crowned with a forest of ancient baobabs. Four pavilions provide casual meals, refreshing drinks and suntanning requisites. Lower down, a second pool—the Royal Baths—has a spectacular view across the Valley of Waves.

GOLF AND CROCODILES

Natural bushveld terrain and rock features, stunning fairways, challenging water hazards, amazing views—and a crocodile pool at hole 13: these are some of the unique attractions at the second, and newest, golf course at the Sun City resort. The 18-hole, 72-par, desert-style course covers 55 hectares and has been designed by the Gary Player Design Company. Each hole has four tees, giving a course length of between 5 400 and 6 900 metres. There is also a practice area incorporating both target greens and practice greens, and a noncontinuous golf-cart path.

Tumbles of honey-coloured stones, mellowing under the sun, decorate a landscape of Palace towers and a club-house apparently restored from an ancient ruin (right). On the golf course, crocodiles are a permanent hazard at hole 13 (left).

Wherever you stand and look about you at The Palace, there are unusual vistas. Interleaved, faux elephant tusks provide a framework for one of the lovely towers outlined against the blue horizon (below).

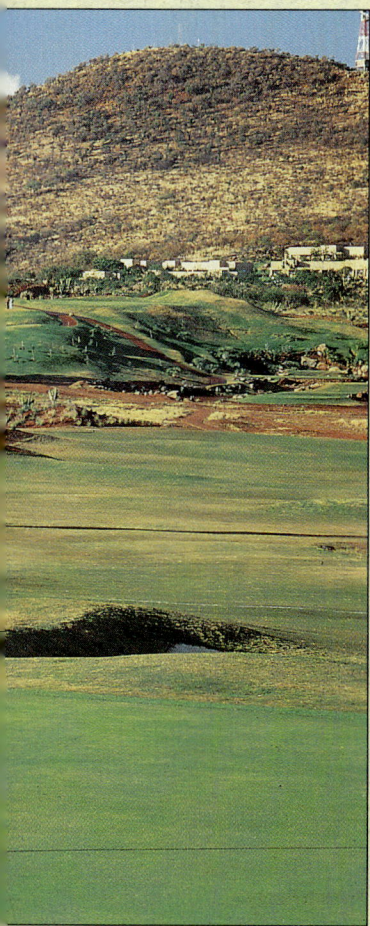

GONG OF THE
SUN LION

THIS MIGHTY GONG USED TO
BOOM OVER THE CITY REGULATING
THE LIVES OF THE PEOPLE
THE GONG OF THE SUN LION
SOUNDED ITS WARNING AS THE
ANCIENTS BRAVELY MOVING IT TO
TO THE SAFETY OF THE ROYAL
ARENA ONLY MOMENTS BEFORE AN
EARTHQUAKE DESTROYED THEIR
DWELLING

FOREST MEANDERS

A rare and beautiful landscape fills The Lost City. Imagination and fantasy have been blended with exceptional horticultural skills to create a world of water and wonder which was two years in the making. More than one and a half million plants, trees, shrubs and ground covers were planted over 25 hectares. The area has 22 different subdivisions, including a rich, tropical section with ebony, fluted milkwood, red beech and African flame trees. This gives way to mist forest; swampy areas that are home to carnivorous plants; then increasingly drier vegetation (affectionately dubbed 'the lunar collection') as the gardens approach the natural African environment on the fringes. Some 10 000 orchids dangle from the forest canopy. There are groves of majestic kiaat, tall stately palms, and centuries-old baobabs with trunks up to six metres in diameter. Through it all meander watercourses, cascades, lakes and footpaths, inviting visitors to explore the hidden secrets of this African paradise.

The faux-stone dome of the ancient Observatory (below, and centre, bottom), now used as a refreshment bar for visitors to the Valley of Waves, still bears the carved incisions of a star chart used by the seers of the Valley's original civilization. A dramatic rope Swing Bridge (above) spans a section of the tangled forest.

Today, all guests at The Palace are welcome to climb the Royal Staircase to the imposing East Gate of The Palace (above), once reserved only for those of royal blood. The steps are intersected by a small stream of dancing water, and lit at night by flickering gas sconces. Rising through constantly changing vistas of tall, tropical forest and waterways, the stairway offers glimpses of the imposing Gong of the Sun Lion (far left, bottom), the hippo canyon and a crocodile river.

An amphi-theatre, evocative of those in ancient Greece and remarkably intact despite earthquake and winds, lies open to the skies (above). The sparkling waters of the Royal Baths are overlooked by ruins of times past (left).

THE ROYAL ARENA

The earthquake-ravaged Royal Arena still stands as a centre of entertainment for the people, despite its tumbled columns and its weatherworn tiers of seats. One can only speculate on the shows which might have been staged in the Arena, for although the people of this Lost City had a rich culture, they left no written record. But today it is just one of the pleasures enjoyed by day visitors to the Valley of Waves. Close to the Royal Baths and its Observatory Bar on the shaded pool deck, there are cascading waterfalls and lush forests.

Only the brave climb up to the Temple of Courage to enjoy five different spine-chilling rides on near vertical water slides (left). One plunges 97 metres down a rock face at a 63-degree angle and dives underground for part of the journey.

THE VALLEY OF WAVES

The Valley of Waves is an adventure playground from the past. This is because the earthquake which destroyed the ancient buildings, mines and aquaducts has left an unusual legacy for today's holiday-makers. The Wave Pool, for example, which is shaped like a scallop shell and laps a beach of white sand (above), was once the village swimming pool. However, the earthquake released a giant underground geyser just below the rock wall. This now surges to the surface every 90 seconds, creating 1,8-metre-high waves which power across the pool, and are perfect for surfing! So today, surfers and bathers take turns to sport in the crystal-clear waters (left).

THE VALLEY OF WAVES

Adventure is found everywhere in the Valley of Waves, though some of it, like the Lazy River Ride, can be enjoyed at a gentle pace. Softly flowing shallow water winds for 500 metres through many fun features, and as the intrepid sailors bob around on their inflatable tubes, they can be watched from the alfresco refreshment plateau encircled by the river. Throughout the Valley of Waves, there are 13 major waterfalls, 20 cascades, two mountain rivers and six wetland areas. Together with three separate lakes and the various swimming pools, they hold a total of 23 million litres and cover 31 500 square metres.

Sun, surf and sand, yet all far from the sea. Shade is found under thatched umbrellas on the beach of the Wave Pool (above), with the towers of The Palace dominating the skyline. For the brave, this is the heart-stopping view over the Wave Pool from the top of a water slide (far left, bottom).

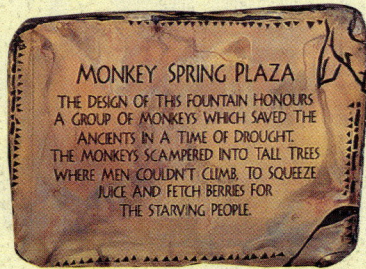

MONKEY SPRING PLAZA
THE DESIGN OF THIS FOUNTAIN HONOURS
A GROUP OF MONKEYS WHICH SAVED THE
ANCIENTS IN A TIME OF DROUGHT.
THE MONKEYS SCAMPERED INTO TALL TREES
WHERE MEN COULDN'T CLIMB, TO SQUEEZE
JUICE AND FETCH BERRIES FOR
THE STARVING PEOPLE.

THE BRIDGE OF TIME

On the far side of the Valley of Waves, a craggy rock face carved in homage to several wild animals hides the amazing fantasy world of the Entertainment Centre, which is linked to the Valley by the Bridge of Time. Nearby, a huge leopard crouches on a rock, guarding the Temple of Creation (below). From here, underground forces (reminiscent of that earlier, destructive earthquake) occasionally explode in a rush of smoke and steam, causing the Bridge to tremble.

Mighty Kong Gates, ten metres high, which once guarded the ancient caverns of the Entertainment Centre from the legendary wild beast, the sassagander, now stand permanently open at one end of the Bridge of Time (above). Elephants sacred to the king of The Lost City still stand with tusks at the ready, forming a guard of honour.

Carvings and statues of leopards, blue cranes, elephants, kudus and monkeys (right) are found throughout The Lost City, but the monkeys had a special place in the hearts of the original people of this Valley. They even built a dramatic Monkey Fountain in thanksgiving to them (far left, top).

Visitors to the Valley of Waves are dwarfed by statues of elephants and the rock carvings on the walls of what is now the Entertainment Centre (above).

The leopard and the elephant (left), which once roamed freely through The Lost City, now live in the adjacent Pilanesberg National Park, but their guardianship of this ancient site continues.

MONKEY SPRING PLAZA

The Monkey Spring Plaza, overlooking the Valley of Waves, is dominated by a beautiful fountain. It was built to honour the monkeys who saved the Valley in a time of terrible drought by picking fruits and berries from the tops of inaccessible trees, and dropping them down to the people below. Four monkeys, with water dripping from their outstretched palms, face the four corners of the earth, and whenever the earth trembles, flames shoot from the bowl above them.

Everywhere in the Entertainment Centre there are technological wonders, from the lofty Hall of Treasures to the thrills of the Jungle Casino (above, and top). *Space-age slot machines and video games fill day and night with excitement, riches and the fulfilment of dreams.*

The Fantasy Jungle Café (left) *is just one of the restaurants in the Hall of Treasures, set amid a rib-tickling fantasy decor enlivened with Balinese hand-carved flowers, petroglyphs created by fibre optics, and hilarious mutations from the animal kingdom like fishalopes, rhinocrocks and elefeathers.*

ENTERTAINMENT FOR ALL

Step across the Bridge of Time and enter the thrilling heart of this extra-ordinary leisure resort: the Entertainment Centre. Besides the royal Banqueting Room which can host over 1 000, the 6 000-seater Superbowl *(above)* has welcomed the Miss World Pageant, entertainers like Frank Sinatra, Elton John, Rod Stewart and Queen, and top international sporting events. Its Dream Machine makes slots punters into multimillionaires at the touch of a button, and everywhere there is fun, fun and more fun.

![elephant silhouette]

ENDLESS ESCAPISM

A dome of rock still arches over the mighty cavern which is now the Entertainment Centre. The roof sparkles with a fibre-optic re-creation of the Milky Way *(above)*, and a five-metre-wide chandelier of cascading leaves lights up a huge gaming pleasureland of merrily ringing slot machines *(below)*, participation video games and imaginatively designed restaurants and bars with menus to match. It helps to be as tall as a giraffe to get the full impact of all the action *(right)*.

The lion may be king of the jungle
(right), but in the Entertainment Centre
fun is also king, for this is where visitors
happily lose themselves for hours in
laughter, luck and leisure.

1 The Cabanas
2 Sun City Hotel
3 Waterworld
4 The Cascades
5 Tennis Courts
6 Gary Player Golf Course
7 Entertainment Centre
8 Bridge of Time
9 Sacred River Ride
10 Valley of Waves
11 Royal Arena
12 Royal Stairs
13 The Palace
14 The Grand Pool
15 Pilanesberg Nature Reserve
16 Lost City Golf Course